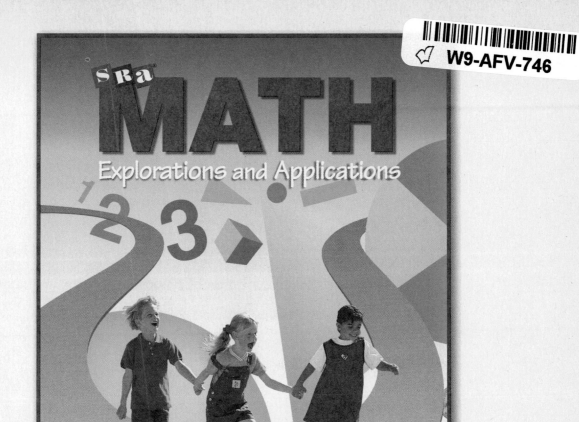

SRA MATH
Explorations and Applications

Stephen S. Willoughby
Carl Bereiter
Peter Hilton
Joseph H. Rubinstein

SRA/McGraw-Hill

A Division of The McGraw-Hill Companies

Printed in the United States of America.

Send all inquiries to:
SRA/McGraw-Hill
250 Old Wilson Bridge Road, Suite 310
Worthington, OH 43085

ISBN 0-02-687851-8

1 2 3 4 5 6 7 8 9 POH 02 01 00 99 98 97

Contents

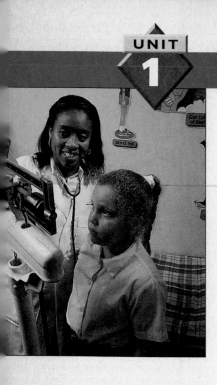

UNIT 1 — Patterns and Numbers

LESSON 1   Comparing Objects 1

LESSON 2   Classifying Objects. 7

LESSON 3   More Classifying 9

LESSON 4   One-to-One Matching 11

LESSON 5   Matching and Comparing 17

LESSON 6   Counting. 21

LESSON 7   More and Fewer. 25

LESSON 8   Counting and Matching. 27

LESSON 9   More Counting 33

LESSON 10   Patterning. 39

LESSON 11   Patterns 43

LESSON 12   More Patterns. 47

LESSON 13   Counting Objects 51

LESSON 14   One More 55

LESSON 15   One Less 61

LESSON 16   0, 1, 2, and 3. 65

LESSON 17   Writing 0, 1, 2, and 3 69

■ LESSON 18   Pennies. 75

LESSON 19   Writing 0–4 79

■ LESSON 20   Pennies and Nickels 85

LESSON 21   Writing 0–6 89

LESSON 22   Writing 0–7 95

■ LESSON 23   Estimating Measures. 101

LESSON 24   Writing 0–9 105

■ LESSON 25   Measurement. 113

■ Application   ● Preteaching   ▲ Revisiting

Contents

■ LESSON 26　More Measurement 117

■ LESSON 27　Measuring Length. 119

■ LESSON 28　More Measuring 123

■ LESSON 29　Probability 127

■ LESSON 30　Graphing 129

◆ **Mid-Book Review** 131

UNIT 2 — Shapes and Graphing

▲ LESSON 31　Pennies, Nickels, and Dimes. 135

　 LESSON 32　Solid Figures 139

　 LESSON 33　Circles and Squares. 143

　 LESSON 34　Triangles and Rectangles 145

　 LESSON 35　More Graphing. 147

■ LESSON 36　Making Predictions 149

● LESSON 37　One Half 151

　 LESSON 38　Numbers 11–19 153

　 LESSON 39　Numbers 20–29 157

■ LESSON 40　Using a Calendar. 159

■ LESSON 41　Sequencing Events 161

■ LESSON 42　Ordinal Position 163

■ LESSON 43　More and Less Time. 167

■ LESSON 44　Day and Night 171

■ LESSON 45　Telling Time 173

■ LESSON 46　Reading Clocks. 175

　 LESSON 47　Graphs. 177

■ LESSON 48　Map Reading 179

■ Application　● Preteaching　▲ Revisiting

Contents

LESSON 49   Introducing Addition. 185

LESSON 50   More Addition 189

LESSON 51   Introducing Subtraction 195

LESSON 52   More Subtraction 199

LESSON 53   Addition and Subtraction 205

LESSON 54   Add or Subtract 207

LESSON 55   Word Problems 211

LESSON 56   Number Combinations 213

● LESSON 57   Division Readiness 215

LESSON 58   Counting by Inference 217

● LESSON 59   Multiplication Readiness 219

LESSON 60   Making Graphs 221

◆   **Book Test** 223

■ Application   ● Preteaching   ▲ Revisiting

Name _____

Comparing Objects

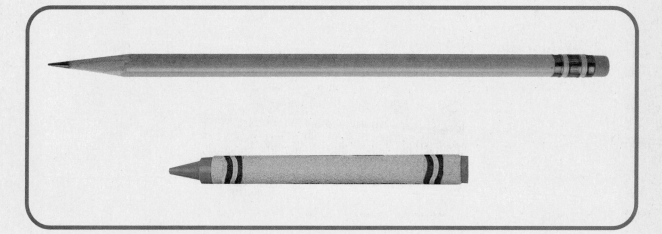

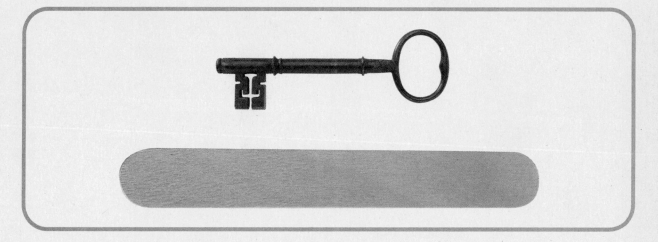

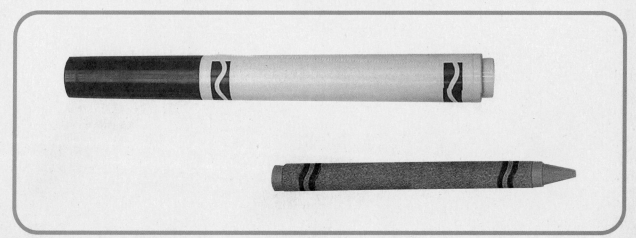

NOTE TO HOME
Students compare lengths.

Name _____

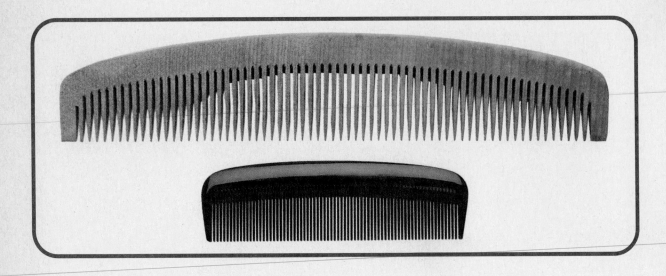

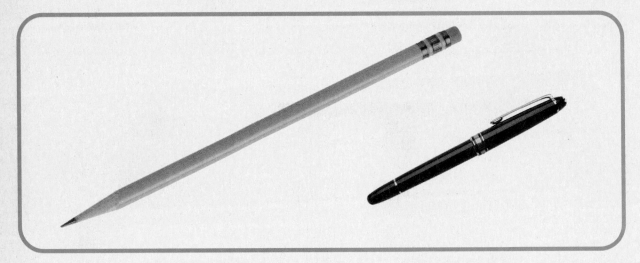

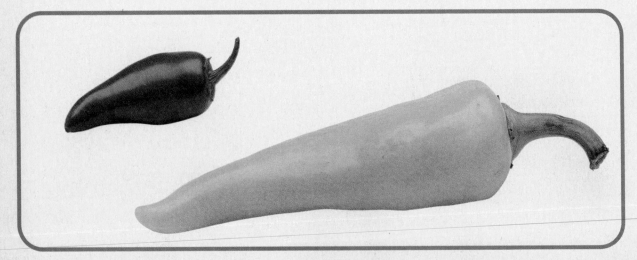

NOTE TO HOME
Students compare lengths.

Name _____

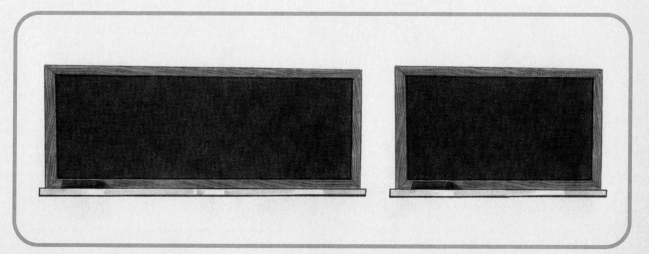

Name _____

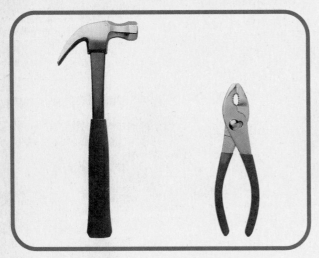

NOTE TO HOME
Students compare heights.

Name _____

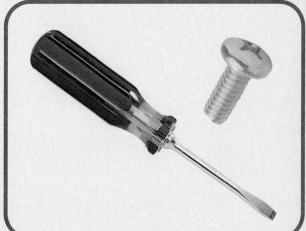

NOTE TO HOME
Students compare weights.

Name _____

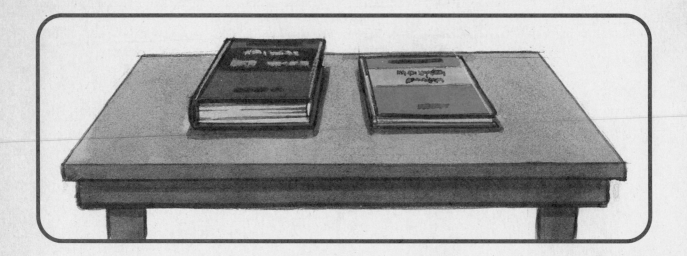

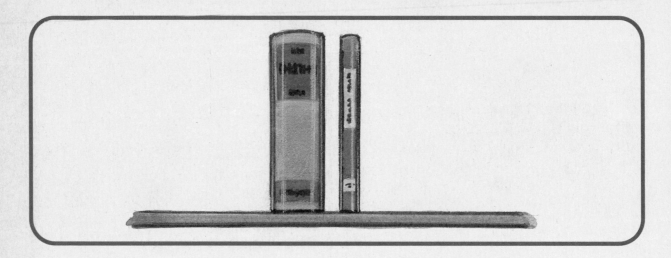

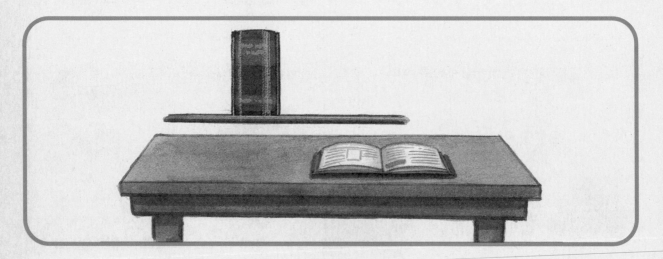

NOTE TO HOME
Students compare thicknesses.

Name _____

Classifying Objects

NOTE TO HOME
Students classify objects.

Name _____

NOTE TO HOME
Students practice classifying.

More Classifying

NOTE TO HOME
Students classify objects.

Name _____

NOTE TO HOME
Students practice classifying objects.

Name _____

More and Fewer

NOTE TO HOME
Students count objects and identify the
picture with more objects.

Name _____

NOTE TO HOME
Students count objects and identify
the picture with fewer objects.

Name _____

Counting and Matching

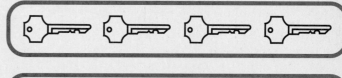
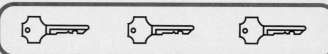

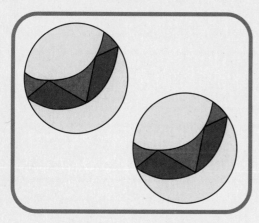

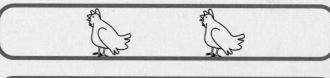

NOTE TO HOME
Students count the number of objects on the left and then draw a line between the two sets that have the same number of objects. Students count to check then color the objects.

Name _____

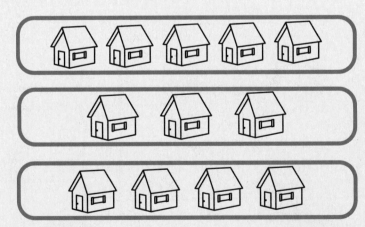

NOTE TO HOME
Students count the number of objects on the left and then draw a line between the two sets that have the same number of objects. Students count to check then color the objects.

28 • Patterns and Numbers

◆ LESSON 8 Counting

Name _____

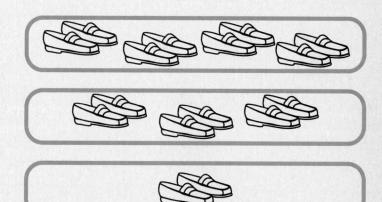

NOTE TO HOME
Students count the number of objects on
the left and then draw a line between the
two sets that have the same number of
objects. Students count to check then color
the objects.

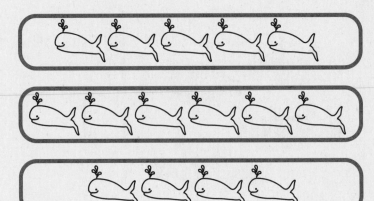

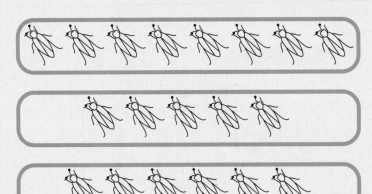

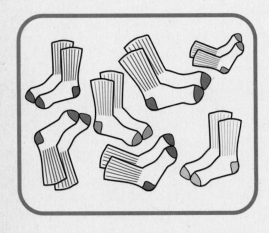

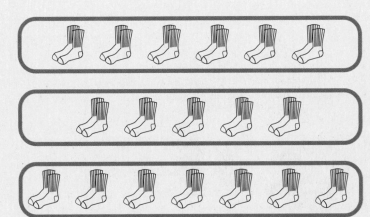

NOTE TO HOME
Students count the number of objects
on the left and then draw a line
between the two sets that have the
same number of objects. Students
count to check then color the objects.

Name _____

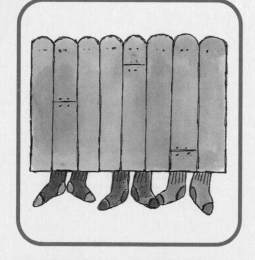

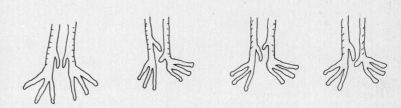

NOTE TO HOME
Students count the objects on the left and
then determine by inference the number of
objects at the right to color.

Name _____

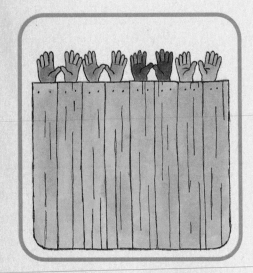

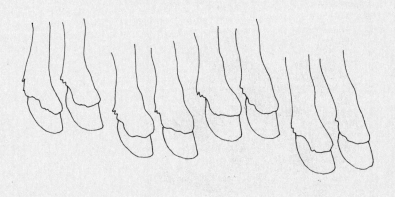

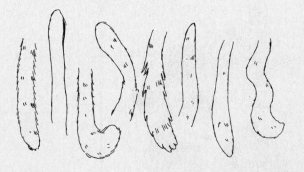

NOTE TO HOME
Students count the objects on the left and then determine by inference the number of objects at the right to color.

Name _____

More Counting

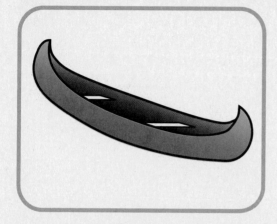

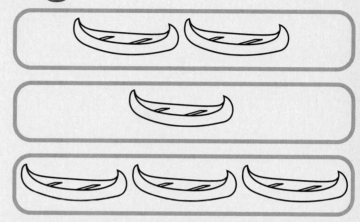

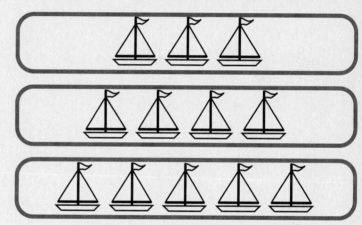

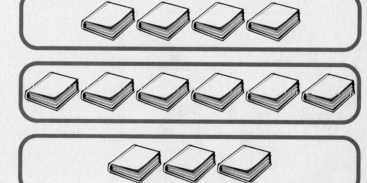

NOTE TO HOME
Students count the number of objects on the left and
then draw a line between the two sets that have the
same number of objects. Students count to check then
color the objects.

Unit 1   Lesson 9 • **33**

Name _____

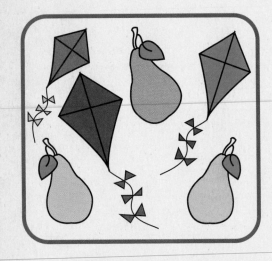

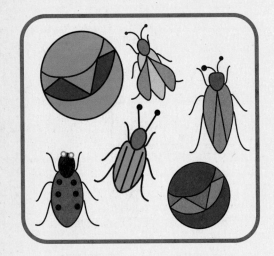

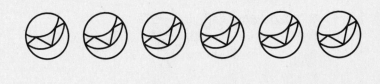

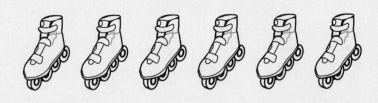

NOTE TO HOME

Students identify the objects on the right, count the number of those objects in the box on the left, and then color the same number of objects at the right.

Name _____

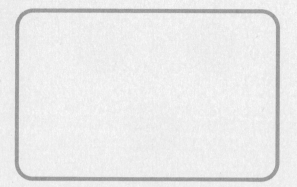

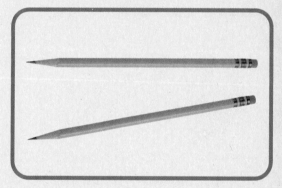

NOTE TO HOME
Students count the objects in each box
on the left, then draw a line to the box
at the right that has the same number of
objects.

Name _____

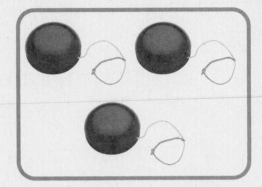

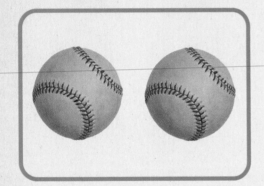

NOTE TO HOME
Students count the objects in each box on the left, then draw a line to the box at the right that has the same number of objects.

Name _____

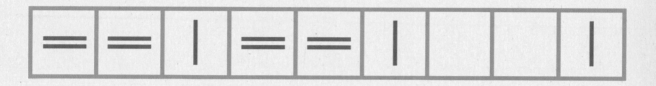

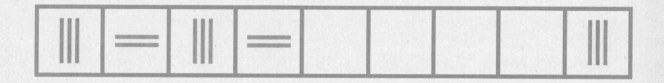

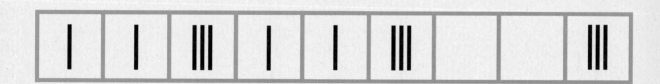

NOTE TO HOME
Students complete patterns.

Name _____

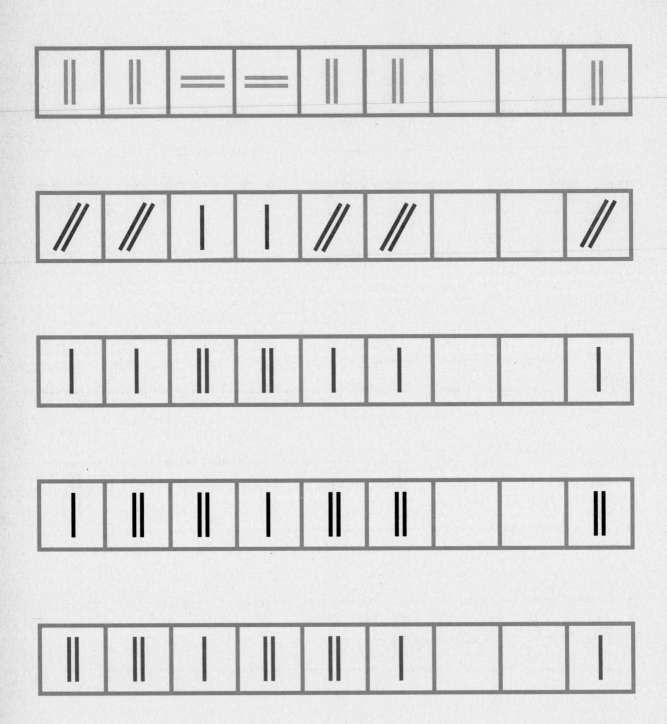

NOTE TO HOME
Students complete patterns.

Name _____

NOTE TO HOME
Students extend the pattern by drawing the
appropriate shape.

Unit 1   Lesson 11 • **45**

Name _____

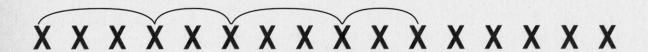

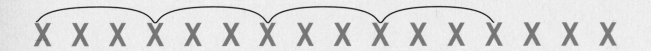

NOTE TO HOME
Students continue the line by extending the pattern.

Name _____

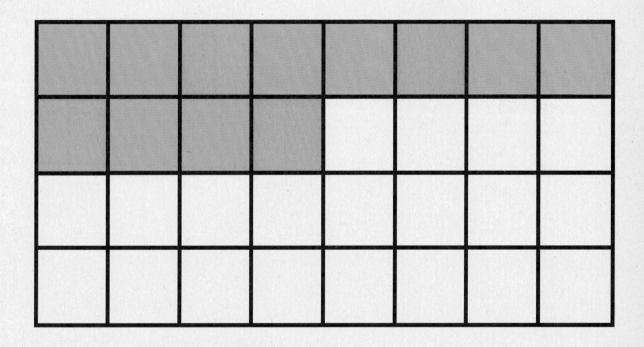

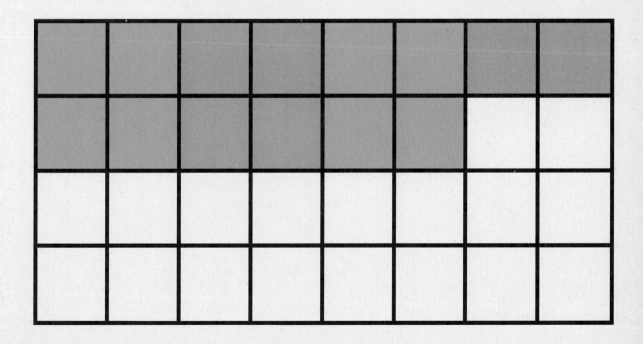

NOTE TO HOME
Students continue to practice identifying and completing patterns. Note that the pattern continues on more than one line.

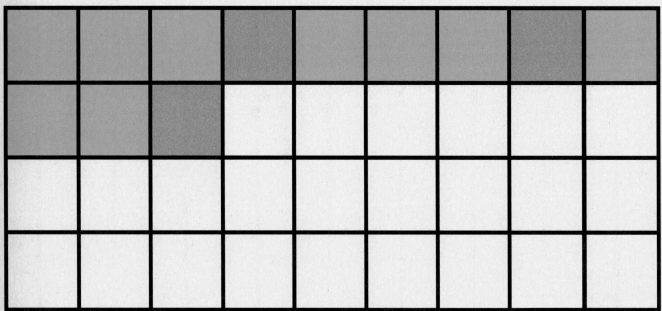

NOTE TO HOME
Students continue to practice identifying
and completing patterns.

Name _____

Counting Objects

NOTE TO HOME
Students count the objects on the left and then
color the same number of objects at the right.

Name _____

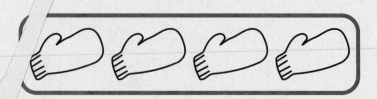

NOTE TO HOME
Students count the objects on the right, count the number of those objects in the box on the left, and then color the same number of objects at the right.

Name _____

One More

NOTE TO HOME
Students draw a line from each large box on the left
to the small box at the right that contains one more.

Name _____

 NOTE TO HOME
Students draw a line from each large box on the left
to the small box at the right that contains one more.

◆ LESSON 14　One More

Name _____

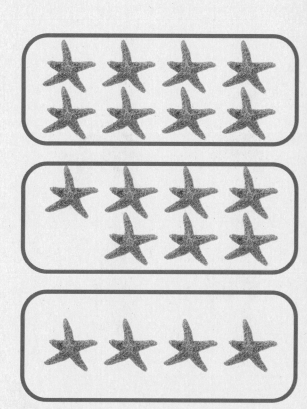

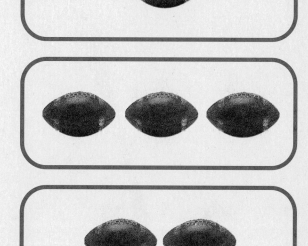

NOTE TO HOME
Students draw a line from each large box on the left to
the small box at the right that contains one more.

Name _____

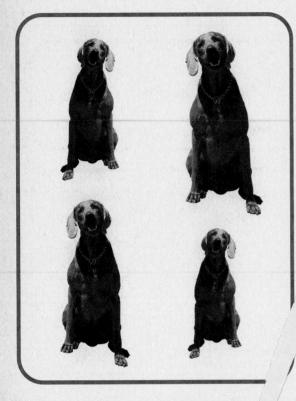

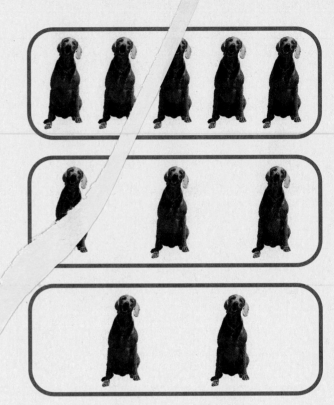

NOTE TO HOME
Students draw a line from each large box on the left
to the small box at the right that contains one more.

Name _____

 NOTE TO HOME
Students draw a line from the large box on the left
to the small box at the right that contains one more.

Name _____

NOTE TO HOME
Students draw a line from the large picture on the left to the small picture at the right that contains one more.

Name _____

One Less

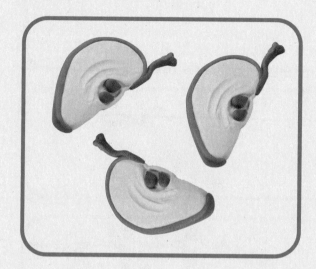

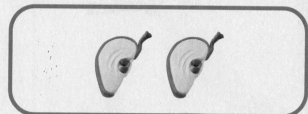

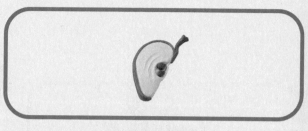

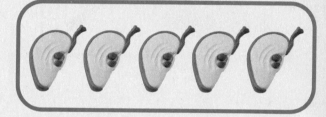

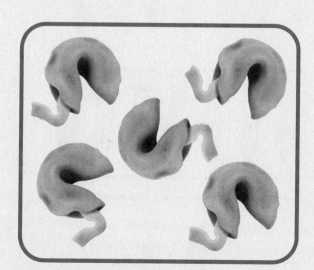

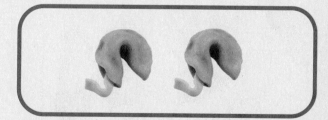

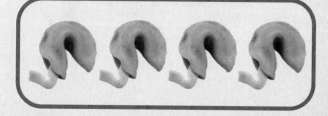

NOTE TO HOME
Students draw a line from each large box
on the left to the small box at the right that
contains one less.

Name _____

NOTE TO HOME
Students draw a line from each large box on the left
to the small box at the right that contains one less.

Name _____

0, 1, 2, and 3

2

3

1

0

NOTE TO HOME
Students draw lines connecting groups of objects
shown in the boxes at the left with the boxes at the
right that tell how many.

Name _____

NOTE TO HOME
Students draw lines connecting groups of objects shown in the boxes at the left with the boxes at the right that tell how many.

Name _____

2

1

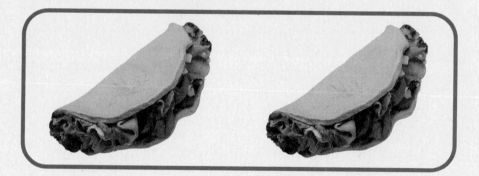

0

3

NOTE TO HOME
Students draw lines connecting groups of objects
shown in the boxes at the left with the boxes at
the right that tell how many.

Name _____

3

2

1

0

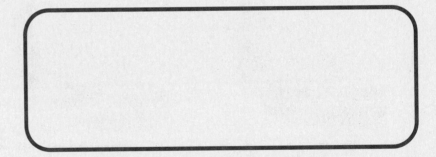

 NOTE TO HOME
Students draw lines connecting the
numerals shown in the boxes at the left
with the boxes of objects on the right.

LESSON 17

Name _____

Writing 0, 1, 2, and 3

2
3

2
1

3
0

NOTE TO HOME
Students trace the gray number on the right that
shows how many objects are in the box at the left.

Copyright © SRA/McGraw-Hill

Unit 1   Lesson 17 • **69**

Name _____

1
2

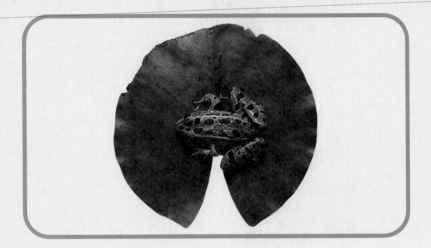

1
3

2
3

NOTE TO HOME
Students trace the gray number on the right that
shows how many objects are in the box at the left.

Name _____

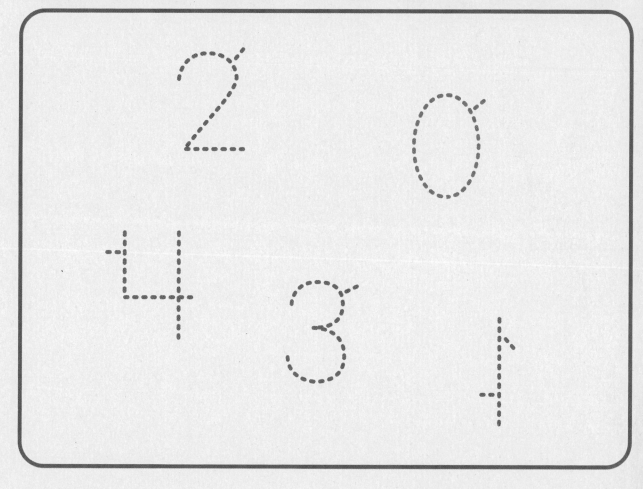

NOTE TO HOME
Students look at the numerals at the top of the page,
then trace over the dots that make the number.

Name _____

1	1		
2	2		
3	3		
4	4		

 NOTE TO HOME
Students trace the gray numerals in the first two boxes in each row. Then they write the numeral in the two empty boxes.

◆ **LESSON 19 Writing 0–4**

Name _____

 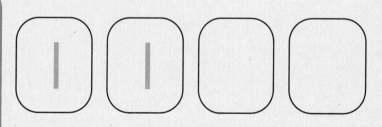

 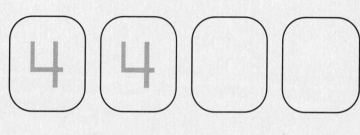

 NOTE TO HOME
Students trace the gray numerals in the first
two boxes in each row. Then they write the
numeral in the two empty boxes.

Unit 1   Lesson 19 • **83**

Name _____

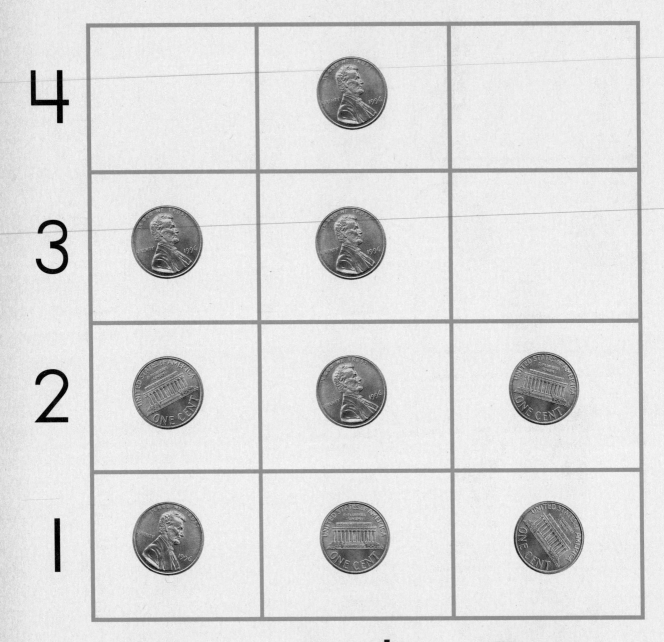

4

3

2

1

Joe   Judy   Dan

 NOTE TO HOME
Students listen to a story and answer
questions using the graph.

Name _____

Pennies and Nickels

NOTE TO HOME
Students draw lines to classify nickels
and pennies.

5 5 ☐ ☐

4 4 ☐ ☐

3 3 ☐ ☐

2 2 ☐ ☐

NOTE TO HOME
Students trace the gray numerals in the first two boxes in each row. Then they write the numeral in the two empty boxes.

Name _____

$\boxed{5}$ $\boxed{5}$ $\boxed{}$ $\boxed{}$

$\boxed{5}$ $\boxed{5}$ $\boxed{}$ $\boxed{}$

$\boxed{3}$ $\boxed{3}$ $\boxed{}$ $\boxed{}$

$\boxed{4}$ $\boxed{4}$ $\boxed{}$ $\boxed{}$

NOTE TO HOME
Students trace the gray numerals in the first two boxes in
each row, then write the numeral in the two empty boxes.

Name _____

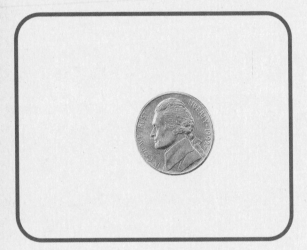 

NOTE TO HOME
Students ring groups that are worth five cents.

Name _____

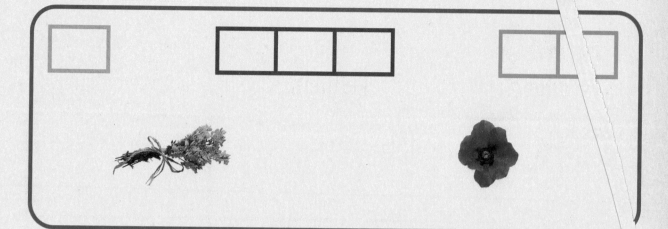

NOTE TO HOME
Students draw lines connecting each object
with the strip above that is the same length.

Name _____

Number Rolled	Tallies	How Many
0		
1		
2		
3		
4		
5		

NOTE TO HOME
Students explore probability using a 0–5 cube or a spinner. They record their results on a chart.

Name _____

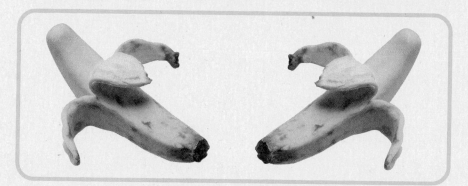

NOTE TO HOME
Students count the objects shown and then
write the appropriate number in the box.

Name _____

5   2   3

7

 NOTE TO HOME
Students compare the height of each object to the units
on the Number Strip. Then they draw a line from each
object to the number at the top of the page that
corresponds with its height and trace the gray number.

Name _____

Estimating Measures

| 4 | 5 | 6 |

| 2 | 3 | 4 |

| 4 | 5 | 6 |

NOTE TO HOME
Students count the number of turtles between the
bird and the mouse. Then students trace that number.

Name _____

NOTE TO HOME
Students count the number of turtles between the
bird and the mouse. Then students trace that number.

Name _____

Measurement

5 6 7 8 9 10

10

NOTE TO HOME
Students judge the height of each object shown by seeing
how many units on the Number Strip correspond to its
height. Students then draw a line from the object to the
number at the top of the page and trace the gray number.

Name _____

q

 NOTE TO HOME
Students judge the height of each object shown
by seeing how many units on the Number Strip
correspond to its height. Students then draw a
line from the object to the number at the top of
the page and trace the gray number.

Name _____

10

9 10 · 3 4

NOTE TO HOME
Students judge the height of each object by seeing
how many units on the Number Strip correspond to its
height, then draw a line from the object to the number
at the top of the page and trace the gray number.

Unit 1   Lesson 25 • **115**

3   5   7

2   3   4

5   6   10

NOTE TO HOME
Students determine how many links long each
object is. Then they trace the gray number below.

Name _____

More Measurement

4   5   6

q

NOTE TO HOME
Students use Number Strips to estimate height.
Then students draw a line from each object to
the numeral at the top and trace the numeral.

Name _____

7   6   5

9

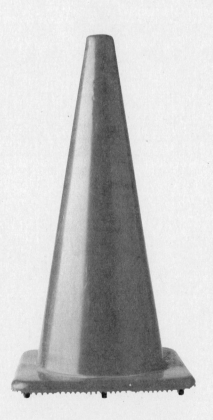

NOTE TO HOME
Students use Number Strips to estimate height.
Then students draw a line from each object to
the gray numeral and trace the numeral.

Name _____

Measuring Length

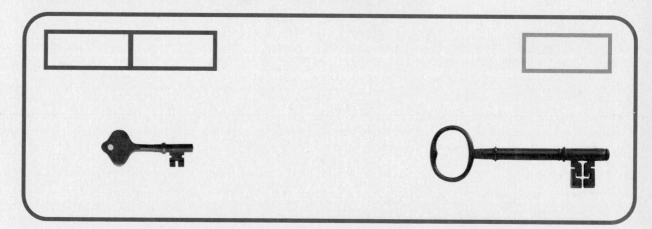

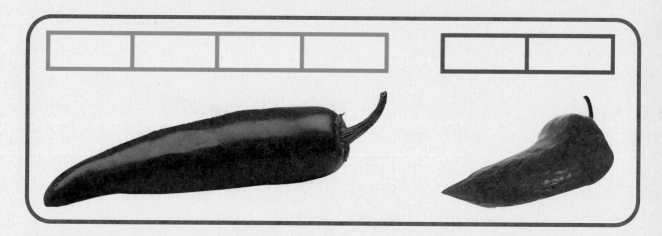

NOTE TO HOME
Students draw a line from the shorter strip to the shorter object and then from the longer strip to the longer object.

Name _____

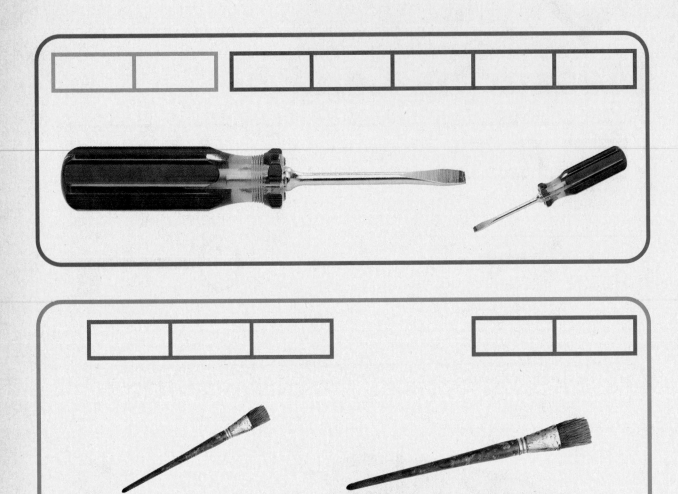

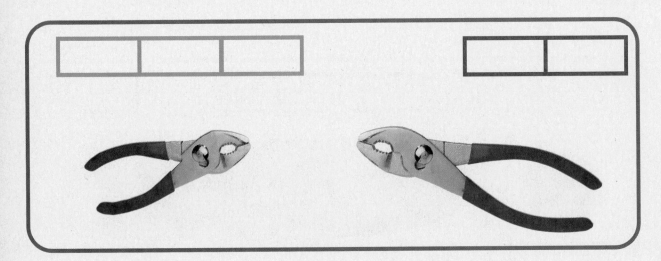

NOTE TO HOME
Students draw lines from the strips to
the objects that have the same length.

Name _____

5   7

4   6

7   9

NOTE TO HOME
Students estimate how many units long each
object is and trace the gray number below.

Name _____

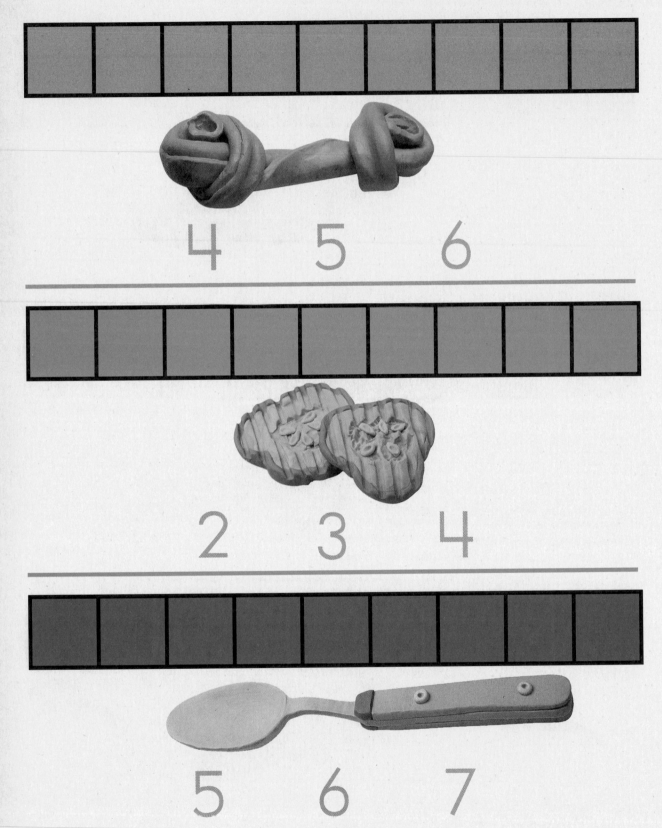

4   5   6

2   3   4

5   6   7

NOTE TO HOME
Students estimate how many units long each
object will be and trace the gray number below.

Name _____

More Measuring

| 5 |
| 4 |
| 3 |
| 2 |
| 1 |

| 7 |
| 6 |
| 5 |
| 4 |
| 3 |
| 2 |
| 1 |

NOTE TO HOME
Students determine how many blocks
high each stack will be and trace the
gray number.

Unit 1   Lesson 28 • **123**

7
6
5
4
3
2
1

7
6
5
4
3
2
1

 NOTE TO HOME
Students determine how many blocks
high each stack will be and trace the
gray number.

Name _____

2   3   4

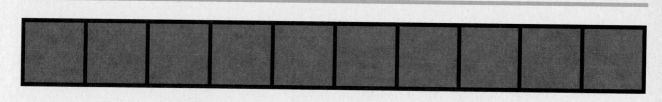

3   4   5

4   5   6

 NOTE TO HOME
Students determine how many cubes long each object
is. Then they trace the gray number below.

Name _____

 NOTE TO HOME
Students count the number of ducks
between the bird and the bug. Then
students write that number.

Name _____

Probability

NOTE TO HOME
Students explore probability using equal numbers of
colored counters. They record their results on a graph.

Name _____

NOTE TO HOME
Students explore probability using unequal numbers of counters. They record their results on a graph.

Name _____

Graphing

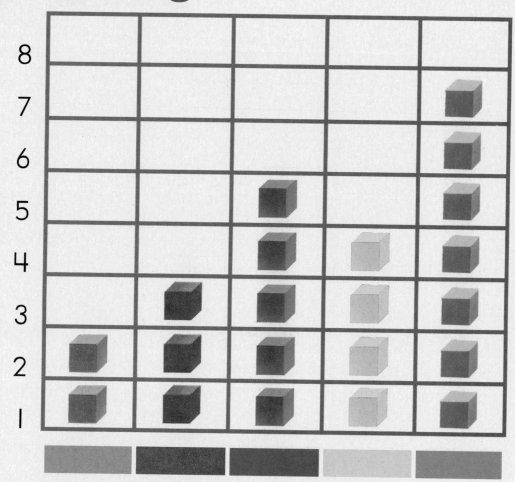

How many?

NOTE TO HOME
Students answer questions using a graph.

Name _____

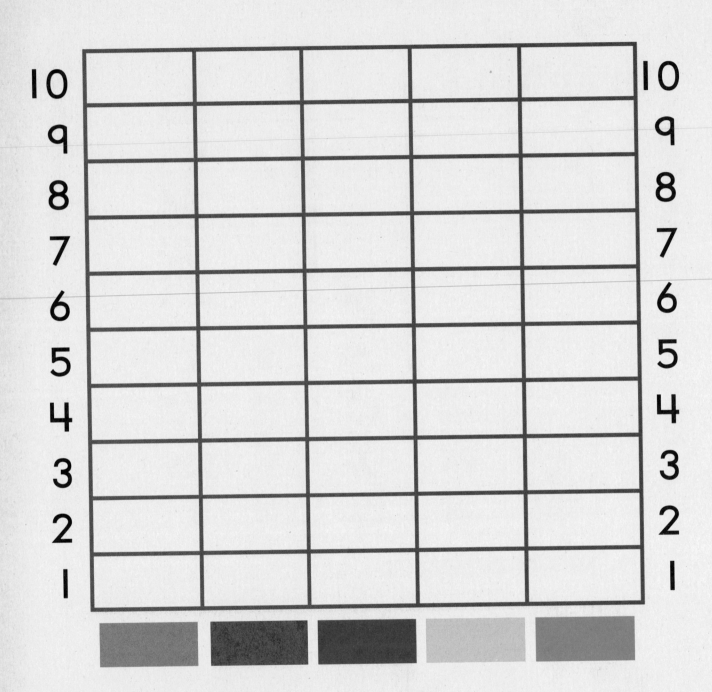

My favorite color is _____

The class's favorite color is _____

NOTE TO HOME
Students collect data and create a bar graph. Then students use their bar graphs to determine the favorite color of the class.

Name _____

Mid-Book Review

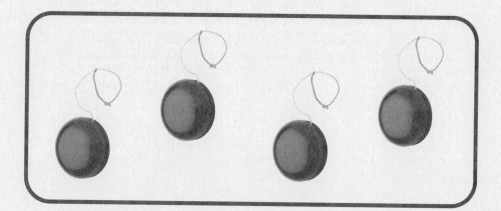

7

4

8

NOTE TO HOME
Students draw lines connecting groups of objects in the boxes at the left with the numbers on the right that tell how many.

Name _____

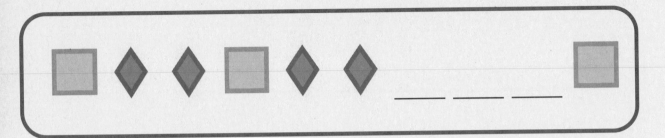

NOTE TO HOME
Students extend a pattern and draw a line to the
picture on the right that shows one more.

Pennies, Nickels, and Dimes

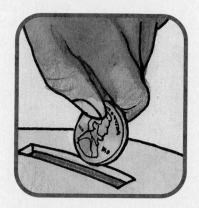

NOTE TO HOME
Students classify pennies, nickels, and dimes.

Name _____

NOTE TO HOME
Students color the number of pennies on
the right that correspond to the amount
of money in the box on the left.

Name _____

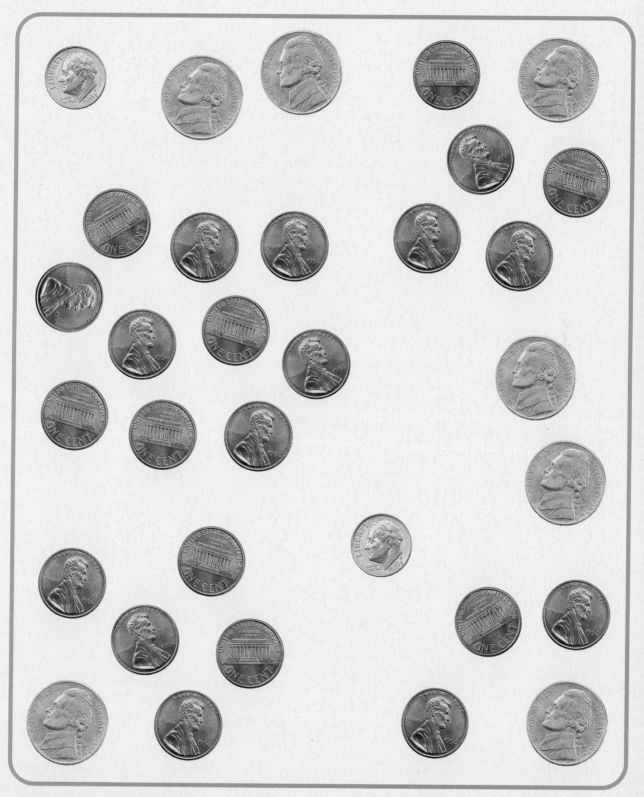

NOTE TO HOME
Students ring groups of coins worth ten cents.

Name _____

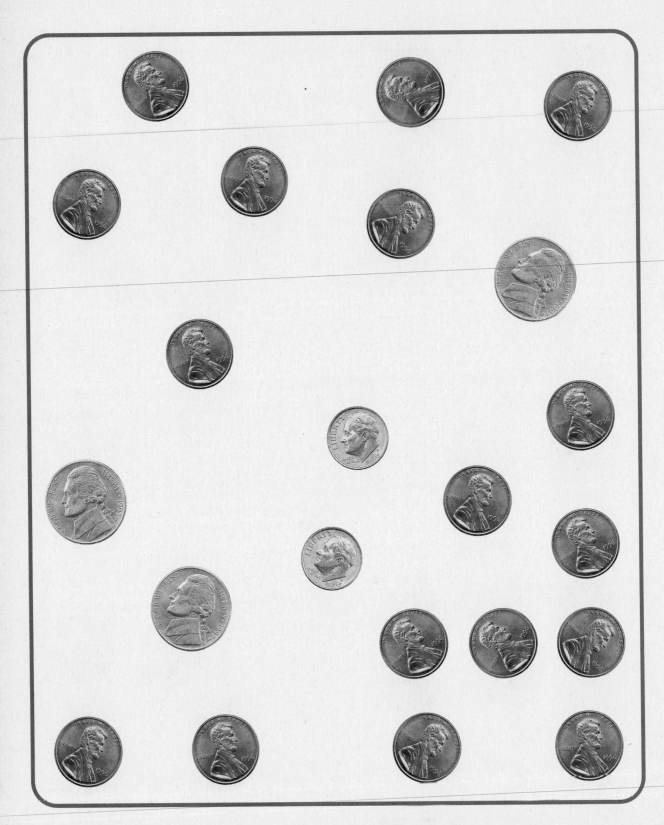

NOTE TO HOME
Students ring groups of
coins worth ten cents.

Name _____

Solid Figures

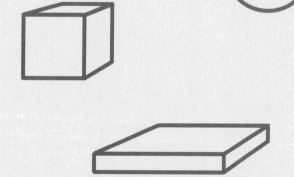
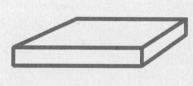
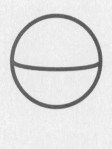

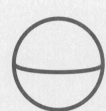

NOTE TO HOME
Students color the spheres.

Name _____

NOTE TO HOME
Students color the cubes blue and
the boxes that are not cubes red.

Name _____

NOTE TO HOME
Students color the cylinders red and
the cones blue.

Name _____

NOTE TO HOME
Students color the spheres red, cylinders orange, cones yellow, cubes purple, and boxes that are not cubes blue.

Name _____

More Graphing

7			▭
6		□	▭
5		□	▭
4	○	□	▭
3	○	□	△	▭
2	○	□	△	▭
1	○	□	△	▭
	○	□	△	▭

Copyright © SRA/McGraw-Hill

NOTE TO HOME
Students read a picture graph.

Name _____

7				
6				
5				
4				
3				
2				
1				
	○	☐	△	▭

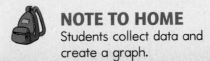

NOTE TO HOME
Students collect data and
create a graph.

Making Predictions

7		
6		
5		
4		
3		
2		
1		
	△	▢

 NOTE TO HOME
Students predict which shape will most likely
be picked from a container.

	△	□
7		
6		
5		
4		
3		
2		
1		

NOTE TO HOME
Students predict which shape will most
likely be picked from a container.

Name _____

One Half

NOTE TO HOME
Students ring the shapes that have two equal parts.

Name _____

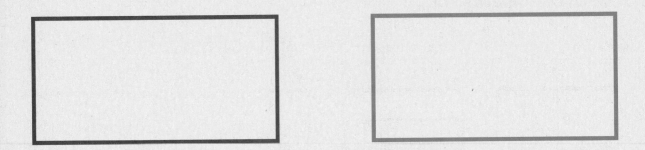

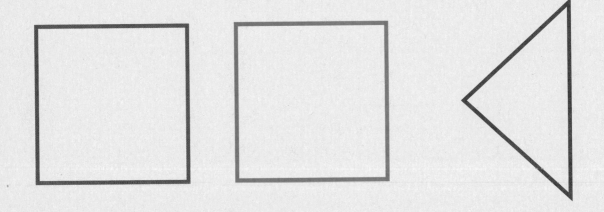

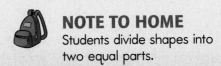

NOTE TO HOME
Students divide shapes into
two equal parts.

Name _____

Numbers 11–19

(11)

(12)

(13)

 NOTE TO HOME
Students color all the pictures showing 11 red,
showing 12 blue, and showing 13 green.

4

5

6

10   10   10

16

14

15

NOTE TO HOME
Students color all the pictures showing
14 yellow, showing 15 purple, and
showing 16 orange.

Name _____

18

7

8

9

10   10   10

17   19

NOTE TO HOME
Students color all the pictures showing 17 green,
showing 18 orange, and showing 19 blue.

Name _____

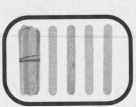

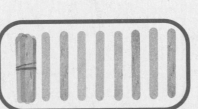

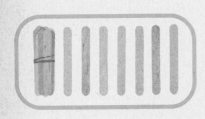

Name _____

Numbers 20–29

 29

23

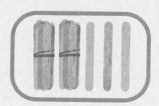

20

28

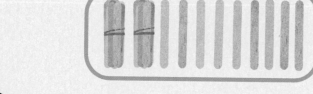

22

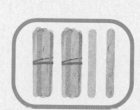

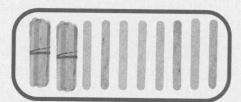

25

Copyright © SRA/McGraw-Hill

 NOTE TO HOME
Students color the pictures and the numbers
that tell how many of the same color.

Name _____

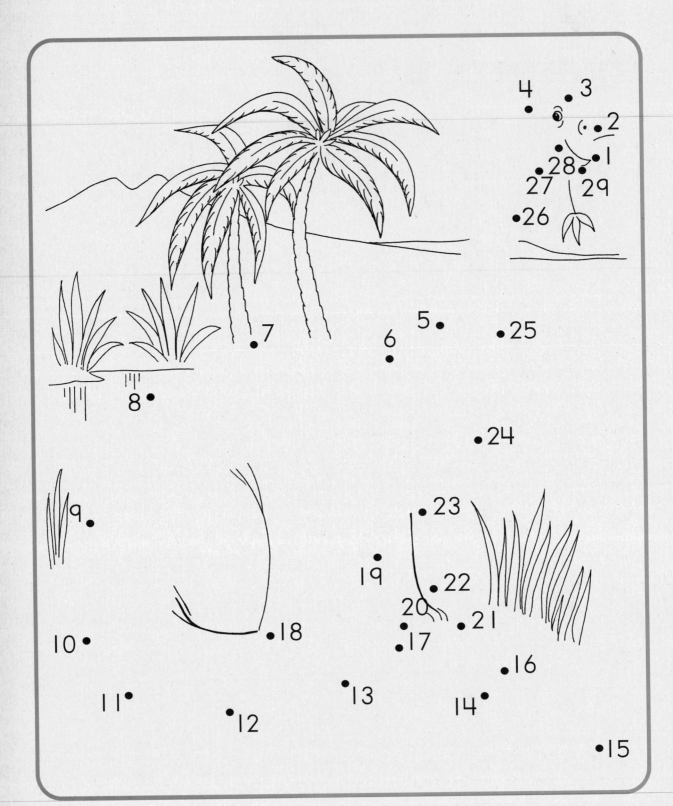

NOTE TO HOME
Students connect the dots to make a picture.

Name _____

Using a Calendar

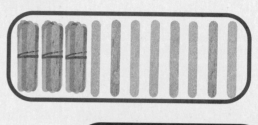

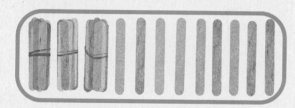

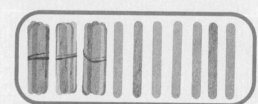

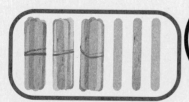

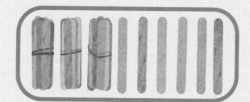

NOTE TO HOME
Students color the pictures and the numbers
that tell how many of the same color.

Name _____

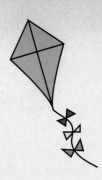

March

Sunday	Monday	Tuesday	Wednesday	Thursday	Friday	Saturday
						1
2	3			6		8
9		11	12	13	14	15
16	17	18	19	20	21	22
23	24	25	26	27	28	29
30	31					

NOTE TO HOME
Students trace and write the numbers
to complete a calendar.

Name _____

Sequencing Events

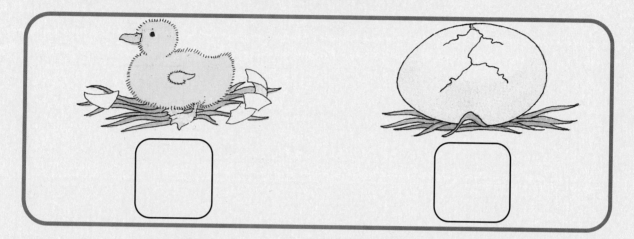

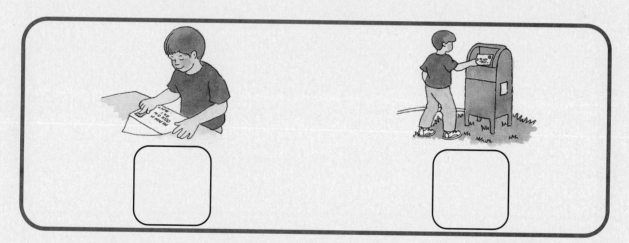

NOTE TO HOME
Students identify what happened first and last
by writing the numbers 1 and 2 to show order.

Name _____

NOTE TO HOME
Students identify what happened first, next, and last by writing the numbers 1, 2, and 3 to show order.

162 • Shapes and Graphing

Name _____

Ordinal Position

NOTE TO HOME
Students color the second elephant blue, ring the third
bee, color the fourth bird red, and color the eighth cat
their favorite color.

Name _____

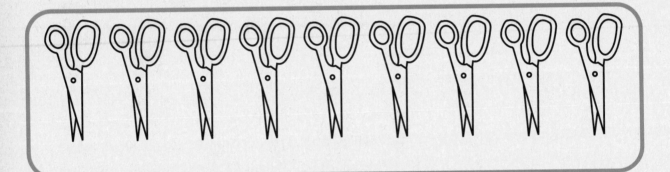

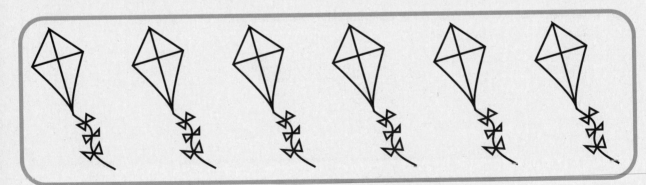

NOTE TO HOME
Students draw a circle around the sixth ring, color the seventh pair of scissors yellow, color the third pineapple brown, and color the first kite purple.

◆ LESSON 42 Ordinal Position

Name _____

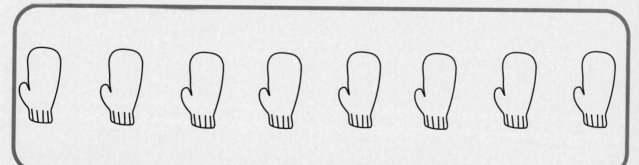

Copyright © SRA/McGraw-Hill

NOTE TO HOME
Students draw a circle on the fifth butterfly, color the
fourth giraffe green, draw a bee on the fourth flower,
and color the sixth mitten blue.

Unit 2 Lesson 42 • **165**

Name _____

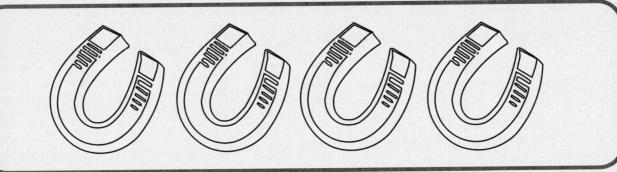

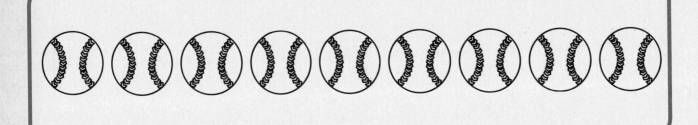

 NOTE TO HOME
Students color the third whale blue, color
the second horseshoe red, ring the eighth
baseball, and color the seventh bee yellow.

More and Less Time

NOTE TO HOME
Students draw an X on the
events that take more time.

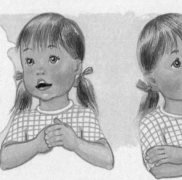

NOTE TO HOME
Students put an X on the events that take more time.

◆ LESSON 43 More and Less Time

Name _____

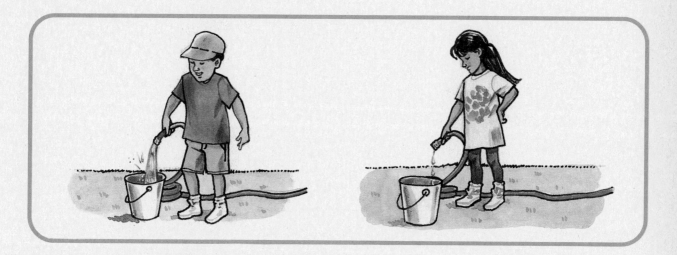

NOTE TO HOME
Students draw an X on the
events that take less time.

Name _____

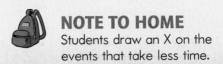

NOTE TO HOME
Students draw an X on the
events that take less time.

Name _____

Day and Night

NOTE TO HOME
Students draw a line from pictures of the activities
that take place at night to the nighttime scene, and
draw a line from pictures of the activities that take
place during the day to the daytime scene.

Unit 2   Lesson 44 • **171**

Name _____

NOTE TO HOME
Students draw a line from pictures of the activities that take place at night to the nighttime scene and draw a line from pictures of the activities that take place during the day to the daytime scene.

172 • Shapes and Graphing

Name _____

Telling Time

 **NOTE TO HOME**
Students fill in the missing numbers on the clock and color
the minute hand red and the hour hand blue.

Name _____

☐ o'clock

☐ o'clock

☐ o'clock

☐ o'clock

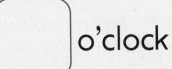

NOTE TO HOME
Students tell time to the hour.

Name _____

Reading Clocks

NOTE TO HOME
Students draw lines between analog
and digital clocks that show the same time.

Name _____

NOTE TO HOME
Students draw lines between analog and digital clocks that show the same time.

LESSON
47

Name _____

Graphs

10			
9	X		
8	X		
7	X		X
6	X		X
5	X		X
4	X		X
3	X		X
2	X	X	X
1	X	X	X

NOTE TO HOME
Students read and interpret a graph.

Name _____

10			
9			
8			
7			
6			
5			
4			
3			
2			
1			

NOTE TO HOME
Students practice collecting and
organizing data to make a bar graph.

LESSON 48

Name _____

Map Reading

NOTE TO HOME
Students listen to the story and draw the
path on the map the character took.

Unit 2 Lesson 48 • **179**

Name _____

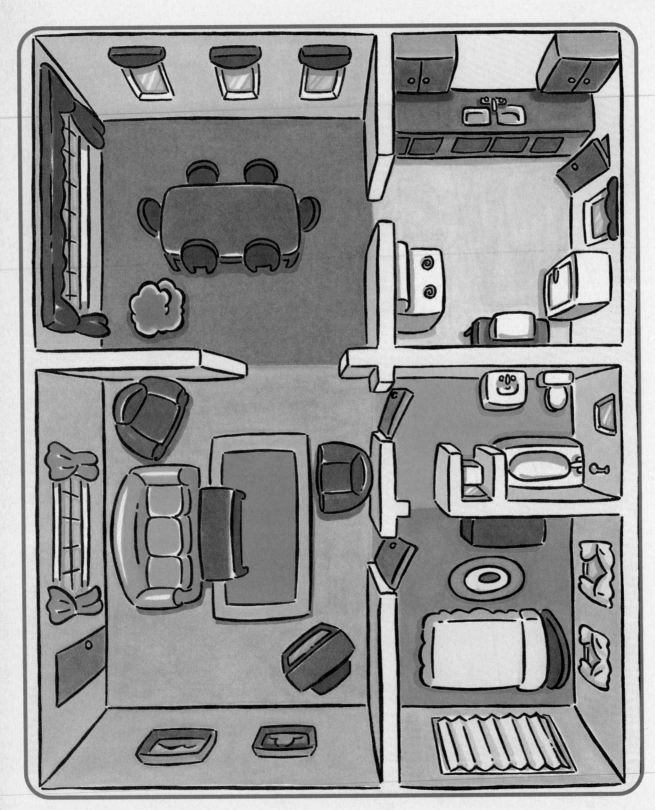

NOTE TO HOME
Students listen to the story and draw the path on the map the character took.

Name _____

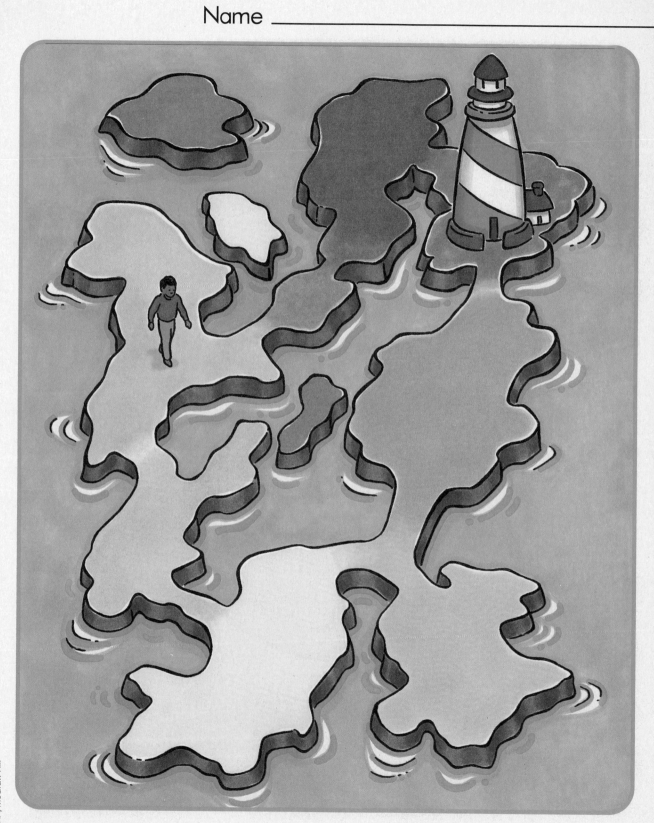

NOTE TO HOME
Students listen to the story and draw the
path on the map the character took.

Name _____

NOTE TO HOME
Students listen to the story and draw the
path on the map the characters took.

Name _____

NOTE TO HOME
Students listen to the story and draw the
path on the map the character took.

Name _____

NOTE TO HOME
Students make a scale drawing of their classroom.

Name _____

Introducing Addition

NOTE TO HOME
Students use the mat to create addition sentences.

Name _____

NOTE TO HOME
Students use the mat to create
addition sentences.

Name _____

NOTE TO HOME
Students determine how many blocks
high each stack will be and trace the
gray number.

Name _____

NOTE TO HOME
Students use Number Strips to measure the distance
around each figure. (Perimeter Readiness)

Name _____

Introducing Subtraction

 NOTE TO HOME
Students use the mat to create
subtraction sentences.

Name _____

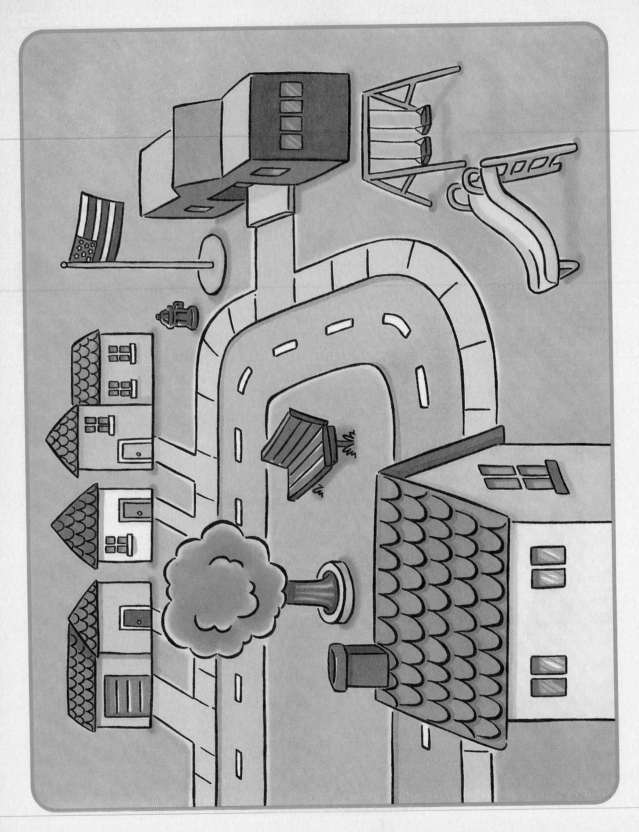

NOTE TO HOME
Students use the mat to create subtraction sentences.

Name _____

$$8 - 3$$

$$3 - 3$$

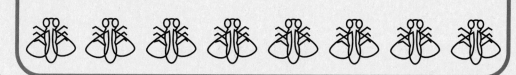

$$6 - 1$$

$$6 - 0$$

 NOTE TO HOME
Students color figures and then draw a slash through
the figures to show the subtraction sentence. They
write the answer in the box on the right.

Name _____

5 − 4

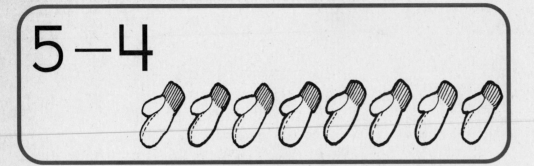

4 − 4

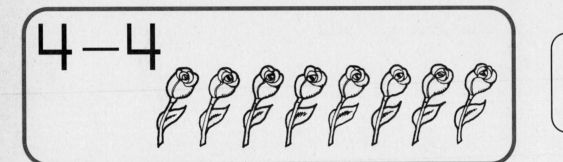

8 − 8

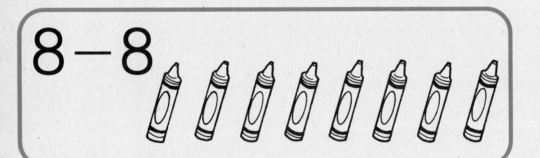

7 − 3

 NOTE TO HOME
Students color figures and then draw a slash through the figures to show the subtraction sentence. They write the answer in the box on the right.

◆ LESSON 52 More Subtraction

Name _____

NOTE TO HOME
Students determine how many blocks high each stack
will be after the blocks are removed and trace the
gray number.

Name _____

8 − 3

5 − 2

NOTE TO HOME
Students listen to a story to determine how many blocks high each stack will be. They write the number on the box.

Add or Subtract

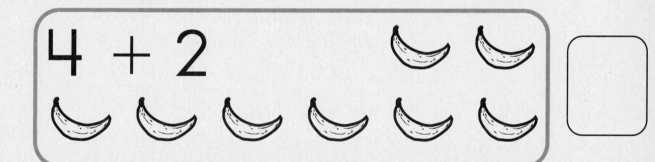

$$6 - 1$$

$$4 + 2$$

$$7 - 3$$

$$6 + 2$$

NOTE TO HOME
Students color figures to show the addition or subtraction
sentence and write the answer in the box on the right.

Name _____

0 + 4

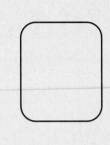

0 + 5

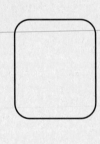

2 + 6

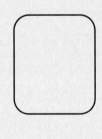

6 − 2

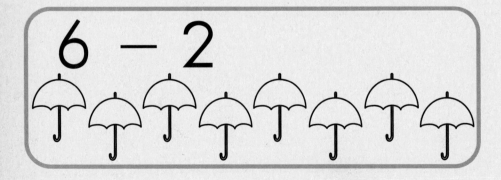

 NOTE TO HOME
Students color figures to show the addition or
subtraction sentence and write the answer in
the box on the right.

208 • Shapes and Graphing

Name _____

 NOTE TO HOME
Students determine how many blocks high each
stack will be and trace the gray number.

Name _____

5 + 3 ☐

8 − 4 ☐

Copyright © SRA/McGraw-Hill

NOTE TO HOME
Students listen to a story and determine
how many blocks high each stack will be
and write the number on the line.

210 • Shapes and Graphing

Name _____

Word Problems

$5 + 2$

$3 - 2$

$7 + 2$

 NOTE TO HOME
Students listen to a story and tell how many
all together or how many are left.

Name _____

7 – 3

4 – 1

6 + 2

NOTE TO HOME
Students listen to a story and tell how
many all together or how many are left.

212 • Shapes and Graphing

Number Combinations

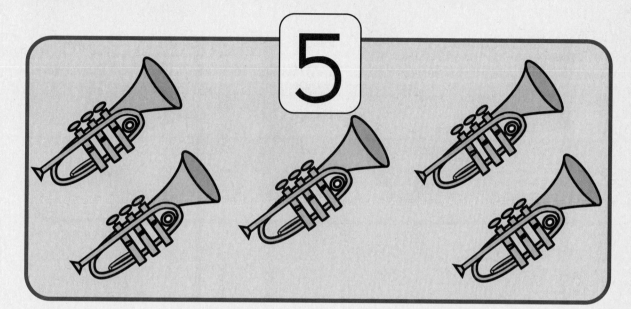

5

7 − 2   4 +

6 −   3 +

5 −   2 +

5 +   1 +

 NOTE TO HOME
Students write the number that is to be
added or subtracted to make 5.

Name _____

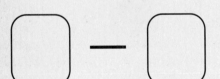 — 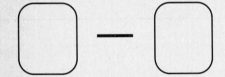   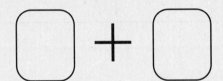 + □

□ — □   □ + □

□ — □   □ + □

□ — □   □ + □

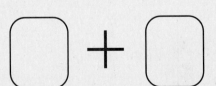 **NOTE TO HOME**
Students write number sentences using different combinations to make 4.

LESSON
57

Name _____

Division Readiness

NOTE TO HOME
Students draw rings around groups of two, count the
number of groups of two, and write that number in
the box.

Name _____

NOTE TO HOME
Students draw rings around groups of three,
count the number of groups of three, and write
that number in the box.

Counting by Inference

NOTE TO HOME
Students determine how many wings go with
the birds, wheels with the cars, giraffe heads
with feet.

Name _____

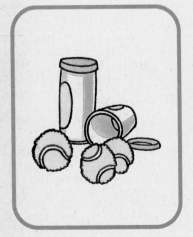

NOTE TO HOME
Students determine how many plants are hidden, how many mittens cannot be seen, and how many balls are in the closed can.

Name _____

Multiplication Readiness

	Mark	Sara	Laura
7			
6			
5			🚗🚗
4	🚗🚗		🚗🚗
3	🚗🚗	🚗🚗	🚗🚗
2	🚗🚗	🚗🚗	🚗🚗
1	🚗🚗	🚗🚗	🚗🚗

NOTE TO HOME
Students read a picture graph and answer questions
about the number of boxes collected and cars collected.

Unit 2   Lesson 59 • **219**

Name _____

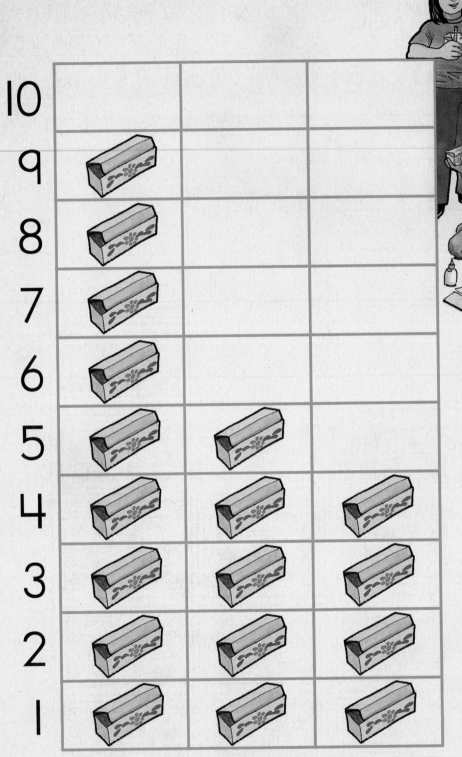

	Miss Laura	Mrs. Abby	Mr. Ebert
10			
9	box		
8	box		
7	box		
6	box		
5	box	box	
4	box	box	box
3	box	box	box
2	box	box	box
1	box	box	box

Miss Laura   Mrs. Abby   Mr. Ebert

NOTE TO HOME
Students read a picture graph and answer
questions about the number of boxes made
and the number of pencils the boxes can hold.
(Multiplication Readiness)

LESSON 60

Name _____

Making Graphs

12				
11				
10				
9				
8				
7				
6				
5				
4				
3				
2				
1	123	ABC	♪♫	✎

NOTE TO HOME
Students read and interpret information
on a bar graph.

Copyright © SRA/McGraw-Hill

Unit 2 Lesson 60 • **221**

Name _____

12			
11			
10			
9			
8			
7			
6			
5			
4			
3			
2			
1			

NOTE TO HOME
Students collect and organize
information using a bar graph.

BOOK
TEST

Name _____

NOTE TO HOME
Students color the circles blue, the triangles brown,
the squares yellow, and the rectangles orange.

Name _____

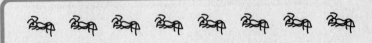

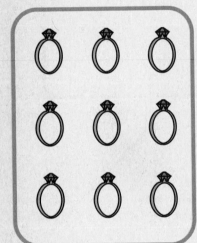

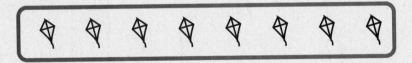

NOTE TO HOME
Students count the objects on the left and then find the set at the right that has the same number and draw a line between the two sets.

224 • Book Test

Name _____

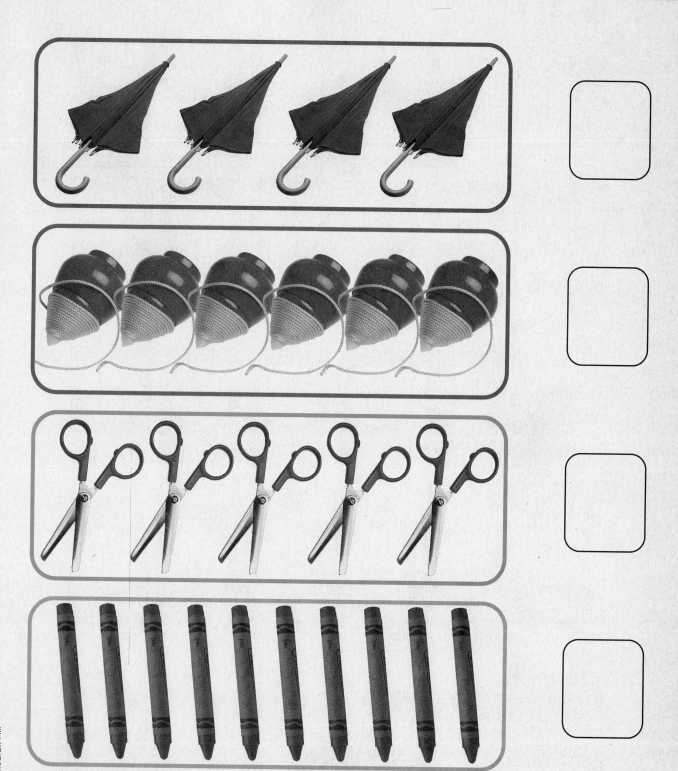

NOTE TO HOME
Students count the objects in each section
and then write the appropriate number in the box.

Name _____

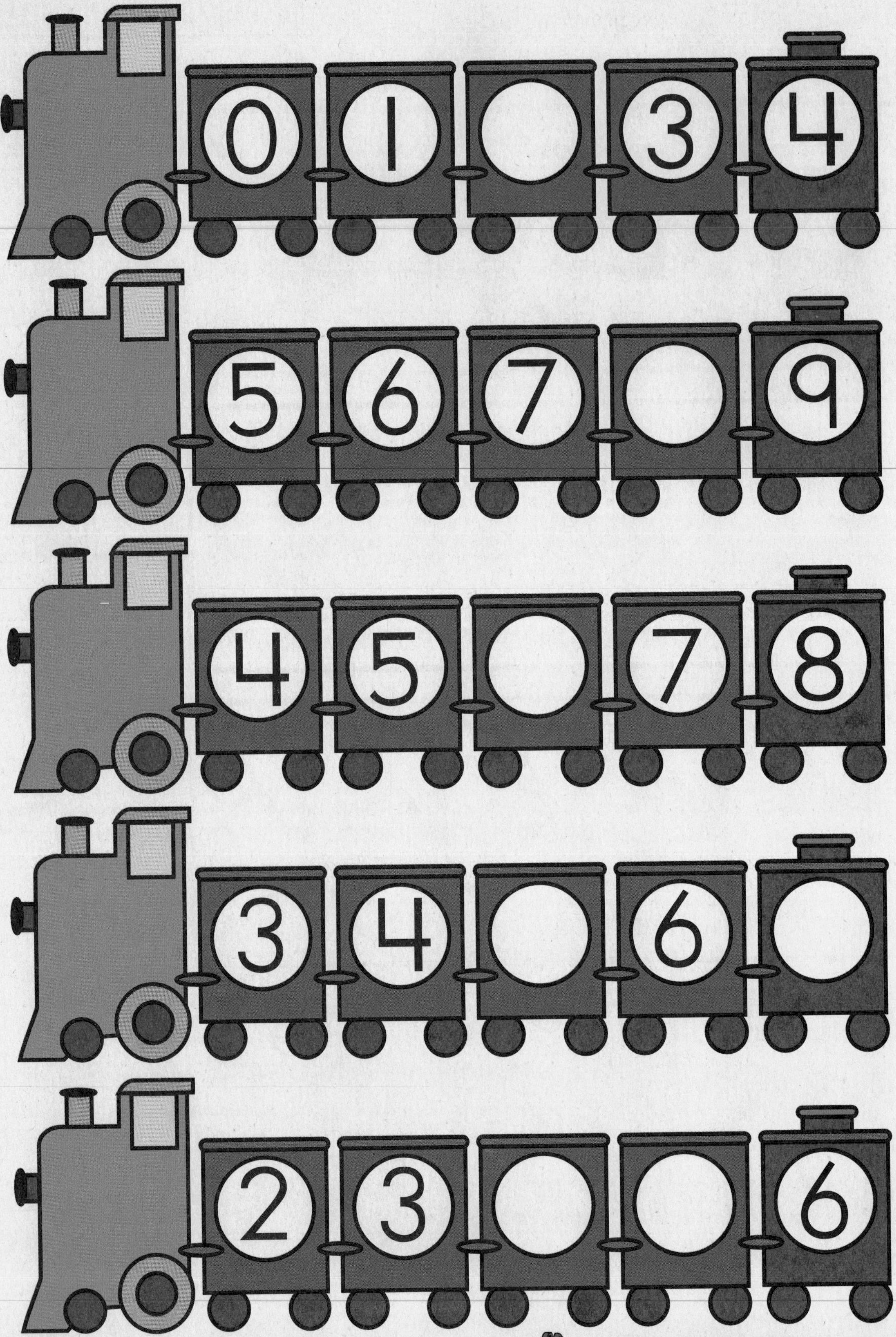

0 1 ◯ 3 4

5 6 7 ◯ 9

4 5 ◯ 7 8

3 4 ◯ 6 ◯

2 3 ◯ ◯ 6

NOTE TO HOME
Students fill in the missing number or numbers in each row.

◆ **Book Test**

Name _____

4 + 2

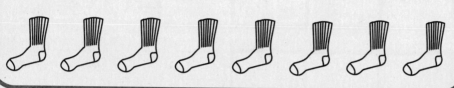

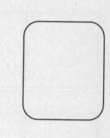

4 − 3

5 − 3

1 + 6

 NOTE TO HOME
Students draw figures to show the addition
or subtraction sentence and write the
answer in the box on the right.

Name _____

Game 1 Trace

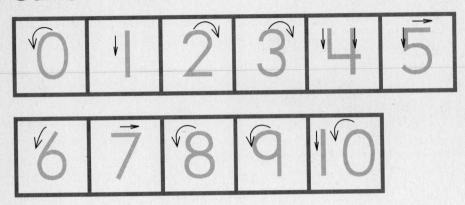

Game 2 Trace

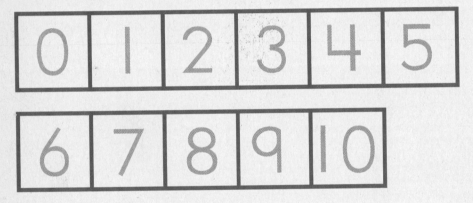

Game 3 Write

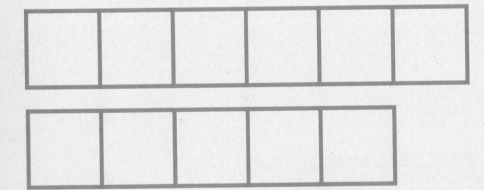

NOTE TO HOME
Students play a game that reviews
writing numerals.